LOL JOKES

PITTSBURGH

GO TEAM!

CRAIG YOE!

arcadia
CHILDREN'S BOOKS

Published by Arcadia Children's Books
A Division of Arcadia Publishing
Charleston, SC
www.arcadiapublishing.com

Copyright © 2021 by Arcadia Children's Books • All rights reserved
First published 2021 • Manufactured in the United States
ISBN 978-1-4671-9815-8

Library of Congress Control Number: 2021932665

All images used © Shutterstock.com; p. 16 jamie cross / Shutterstock.
com; p. 21 f11photo / Shutterstock.com; p. 23 woodsnorthphoto /
Shutterstock.com; p. 28-29 Spiroview Inc / Shutterstock.com; p.
36 EQRoy / Shutterstock.com; p. 68 Rey Rodriguez / Shutterstock.
com; pp. 90-91 Angelina Pilarinos / Shutterstock.com.

Cover illustration: Craig Yoe
Cover design: David Hastings
Page design: Jessica Nevins

Craig Yoe has written a TON of kids'
joke books! Yoe has been a creative
director for Nickelodeon, Disney, and
Jim Henson at the Muppets. Raised
in the Midwest, he has lived from
New York to California and has six kids!

CONTENTS

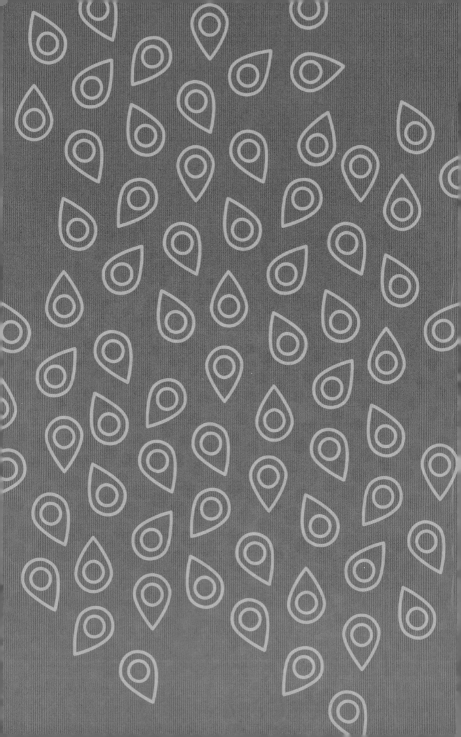

ST⎓EL THIS JOK⎓!

What do you call a sheep in Pittsburgh?

STEEL WOOL!

What kind of rock concerts do steel workers like to go to?

HEAVY METAL!

And so, here's a riddle to give you a smiley face:

Q: How do you measure a riddle's speed?

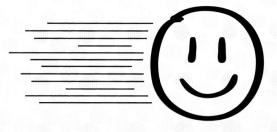

A: In *smiles* per hour!

TIME FOR ANOTHER JOKE!

Timely factoid:
The 60-foot Duquesne Brewery
Clock weighs a ton (for realz)
and is the largest clock face
in the United States.

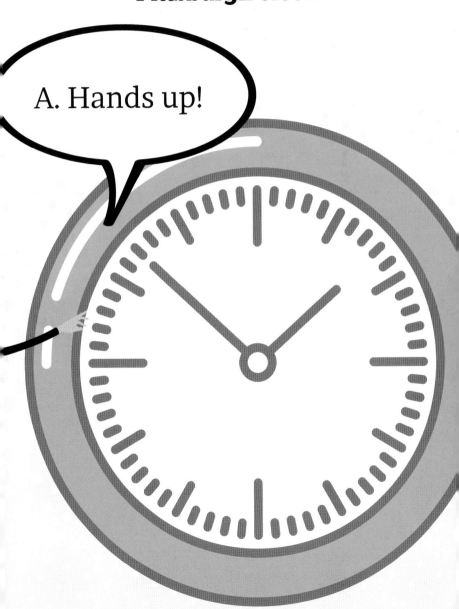

What do you call a bird of prey with a thousand lives?

A millennium falcon!

A STEEP THOUGHT!

The steepest street in the United States is the 'Burgh's Canton Avenue. When you visit the avenue, tell your friend this joke:

WHO'S THERE?
Avenue!

AVENUE WHO?
Avenue heard me knocking and knocking?

What's in the middle of the 'Burgh?

The letter *R*!

WHAT GOES AROUND!

Ferris Factoid:
George Washington Gale Ferris Jr., inventor of the Ferris wheel, lived on the North Side of Pittsburgh!

Ferris was born on February 14, 1859. But it's not just Valentine's Day— it's also National Ferris Wheel Day!

George's invention was first called the Observation wheel because it gave riders bird's-eye views of the landscape below!

Why does going on a Ferris wheel make you important?

You go around in really big circles!

What has one wheel and spins but never goes anywhere?

A Ferris wheel!

ROTFL WITH ROLLER COASTERS

Kennywood's Thunderbolt

Fun Factoid:

The Kennywood Amusement Park, one of only two amusement parks in the United States designated a National Historic Landmark, has not one, not two, not three, not four, not five, but **SIX** roller coasters!

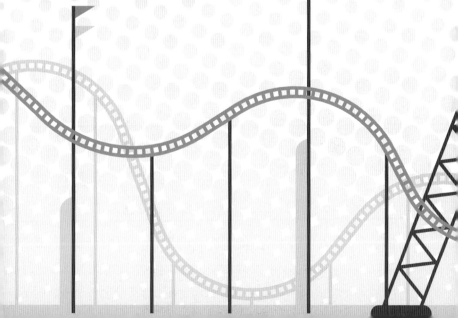

What did the orthodontist do on the Steel Curtain?

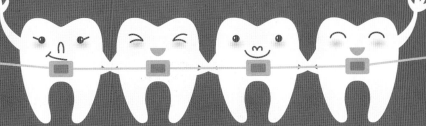

She braced herself!

Smart Factoid:

The Cathedral of Learning on the University of Pittsburgh campus is the tallest educational building in the Western Hemisphere.

Cathedral of Learning

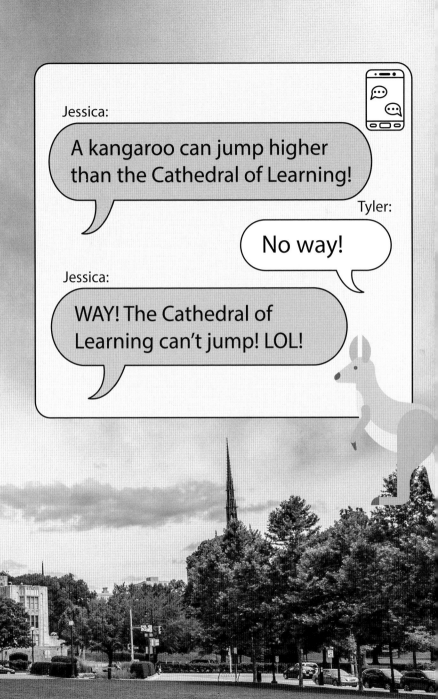

YINZERS ARE *T*-REMENDOUS!

Pittsburgh has a light rail system called the T. It is one of only a handful in the United States that expanded on original trolley car routes from the early 1900s!

(Author's note: I was going to write a good light rail joke here, but I lost my train of thought!)

US Steel Tower

FUN FACTOID

Pittsburgh has 446 bridges, more than almost any other city in the world—including Venice, Italy! *Mama mia!*

What language does a bridge speak?

SPAN-ish!

Andy Warhol Bridge

CHAIR-Y DELIGHT

Pittsburgh citizens save their parking spots by putting a lawn chair in them! (For realz! Some stores even sell special folding chairs that they call parking chairs!)

COLOR ME
HAPPY

FAR-OUT FACTOID:

The brightly colored Randyland has been called "the most painted house in the galaxy." Randyland is the wacky home/art museum of artist Randy Gilson. The artist says, "Break out of your normal! Weird is the new cool!" His website says his museum has a "message of love and happiness most needed in the world today!" Have a short visit: **Visit.** Or a long one: **Viiiiissssssiiiiittttt!**

SOME CLEAN JOKES

Maybe you should read this book:

HOW TO REDD UP

by Phil Thee

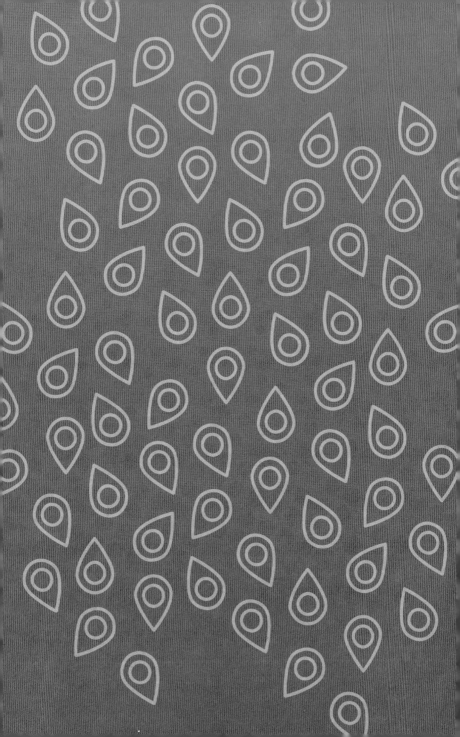

FUN FACTOID

The Steel City's **Carnegie Museum of Natural History** has what could be considered the first specimen of the world's most famous dinosaur, the T. rex! The fossil was discovered by Barnum Brown in 1902 and sent to the American Museum of Natural History. In 1941, it was bought by the Carnegie Museum, where it is still on display. Scientists call this "the holotype of the species." In other words, the Carnegie Museum of Natural History's T. rex is the "gold standard" to which all other fossils of this ferocious meat-eater must forever and a day be compared!

What kind of tests did Andy Warhol take when he was a kid?

POP QUIZZES!

Pittsburgher Jackie Ormes was America's first black woman professional cartoonist!

Jackie Ormes:
Who wants a hug?

Jackie's friend:
**Me!
Put your Ormes
around me!**

PICTURE THIS!

Pittsburgher Charles "Teenie" Harris had big accomplishments! Harris was a professional baseball and basketball player and a photographer who took over 80,000 pictures!

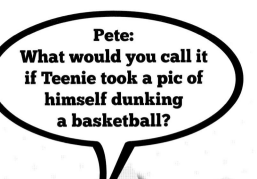

Pete:
What would you call it if Teenie took a pic of himself dunking a basketball?

Michelle:
The perfect shot!

39

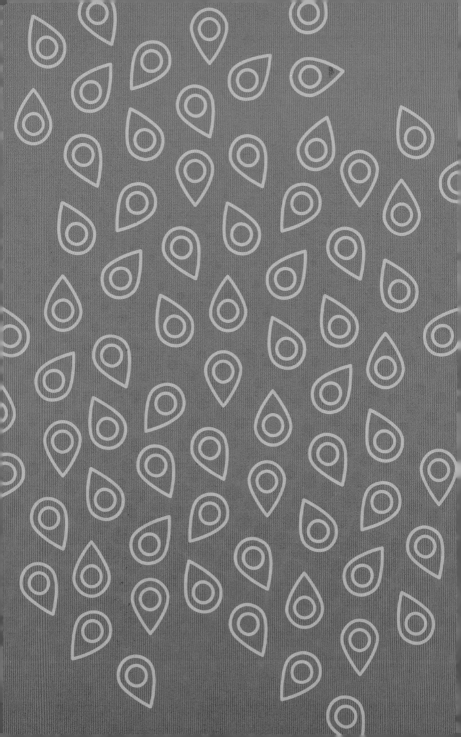

FOR YINZ!

HIRE THIS GUIDE FOR THE BUEL PLANETARIUM AT THE CARNEGIE SCIENCE CENTER:

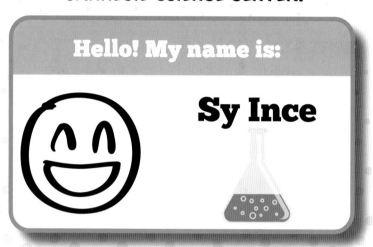

Hello! My name is:

Sy Ince

HIRE THIS GUIDE TO SHOW YOU THE PHIPPS CONSERVATORY AND BOTANICAL GARDENS:

Hello! My name is:

Lily Petal

HIRE THIS GUIDE TO SHOW YOU THE DINOSAURS AT THE CARNEGIE MUSEUM OF NATURAL HISTORY:

Hello! My name is:

Tia Rexx

HIRE THIS GUIDE TO SHOW YOU THE CARNEGIE MUSEUM OF ART:

Hello! My name is:

Art C. Crafty

HIRE THIS GUIDE TO SHOW YOU THE WESTMORELAND MUSEUM OF AMERICAN ART:

HIRE THIS GUIDE TO SHOW YOU THE ANDY WARHOL MUSEUM:

HIRE THIS GUIDE TO SHOW YOU THE PITTSBURGH ZOO:

Hello! My name is:

Sue Keiper

ZOO

BIG LEAGUE FUN

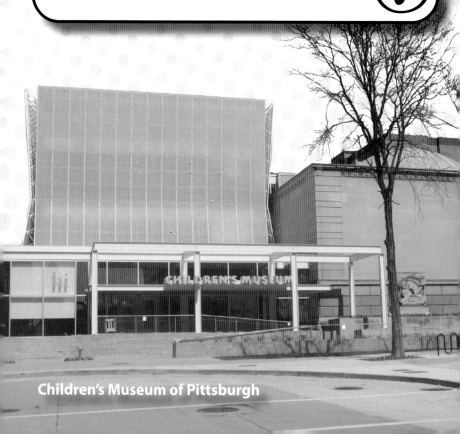

Children's Museum of Pittsburgh

Hank:
I went to the Children's Museum, and now I have my own baseball card!

Aaron:
I always said you were a real card!

The Mattress Factory is one of the coolest, must-see art museums around and is very kid-friendly! In their honor, here's a mattress joke:

What did the mattress say to the spy?

Shhh! I'm undercover!

A WHEELY GREAT!

The world's largest bicycle museum is in Pittsburgh. Bicycle Heaven has 3,000 bikes on display! Let's roll with a couple of bicycle jokes in their honor:

Anna: Hey, your dog was chasing a man on a bicycle!

Marion: Impossible! My dog can't ride a bicycle!

Shhh! Don't tell!

Why did the bike stop halfway home to take a nap?

It was **TWO-TIRED**!

49

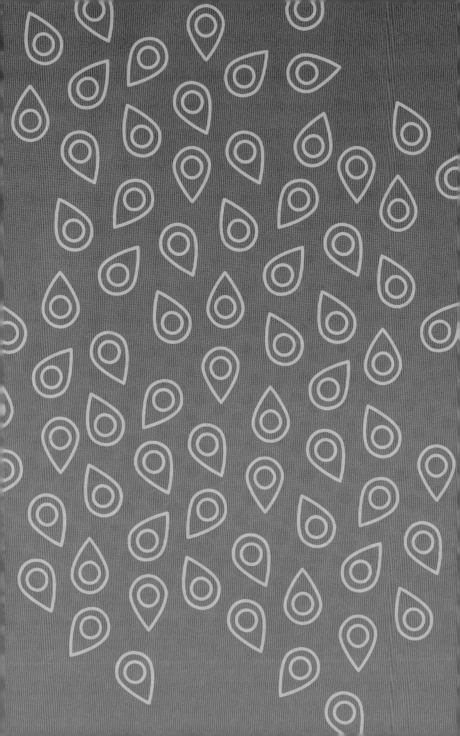

NATURE JOKES

DON'T FORGET TO BE ICE!

Fun Factoid about Pittsburghese!
Instead of "slippery," some
Pittsburghers call ice "slippy"!

What do you call it when ice gets angry?

A meltdown!

What Pittsburgh river is round on both ends and says "Hi" in the middle?

THE
☺-HI-O!

I heard Pittsburgh has two more rivers: the Allegheny and the Monongahela.

Yep! If you're ever in the area, **DROP** in sometime!

FUN FACTOID

You can spot kayakers paddling around the Point, where the Ohio, Allegheny, and Monongahela Rivers meet!

SON OF A FUN FACTOID

Kayak spelled backwards is KAYAK!

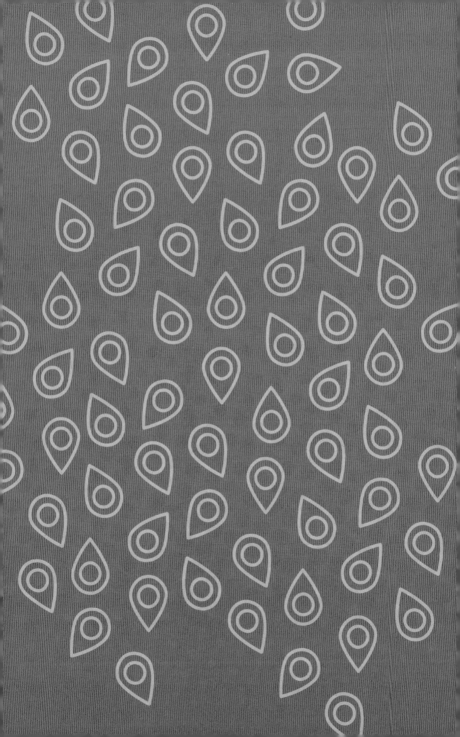

ANIMAL JOKES

What has a beaver's tail, an elephant's ears, and a tiger's stripes?

The Pittsburgh Zoo!

Fun Factoids:
In addition to seeing a Visayan warty pig, a Philippine crocodile, and a pygmy hippo at the Pittsburgh Zoo, you can also see the world's largest rat!

Eeek!

59

Which building in Pittsburgh has the most stories?

The Carnegie Library of Pittsburgh!

For a good–if quiet–laugh, whisper to the librarian and ask to see these books:

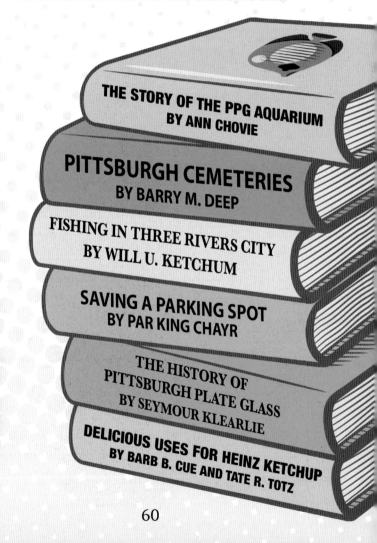

THE STORY OF THE PPG AQUARIUM
BY ANN CHOVIE

PITTSBURGH CEMETERIES
BY BARRY M. DEEP

FISHING IN THREE RIVERS CITY
BY WILL U. KETCHUM

SAVING A PARKING SPOT
BY PAR KING CHAYR

THE HISTORY OF
PITTSBURGH PLATE GLASS
BY SEYMOUR KLEARLIE

DELICIOUS USES FOR HEINZ KETCHUP
BY BARB B. CUE AND TATE R. TOTZ

THE NATIONAL AVIARY
BY C. GULZ AND RAY VINN, WITH PHOTOGRAPHS BY
EARL E. BYRD AND AN INTRODUCTION BY ROB BINN

WALKING THE STEEP
STREETS OF PITTSBURGH
BY IVA BLISTER

HOW TO MAKE A PITTSBURGH SAMMICH
BY COLE SLAW AND CHIP D. HAMM

MORE PITTSBURGH SAMMICHES
BY HOPE N. WYDE

THE PITTSBURGH PIRATES
BY PEG LEGG

STUNNING VIEWS
FROM PITTSBURGH BRIDGES
BY I.C. FARR

DELIGHTS OF THE PHIPPS CONSERVATORY
AND BOTANICAL GARDENS
PAUL N. ATTE

REDDY UP!
BY DALE E. CHORES

BIRD'S THE WORD!

Feathered Factoid:
At the National Aviary, you can go nose-to-beak with over 500 different birds of more than 150 species from around the globe! You can see flamingos, owls, parrots, and even penguins all dressed up in their tuxedos.

Here are some jokes to tell while visiting the Aviary:

Why does a flamingo stand on one leg?

I give up!

Because if it lifted that leg, it would fall over!

62

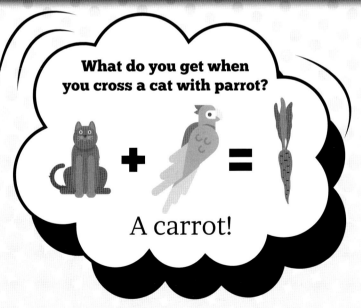

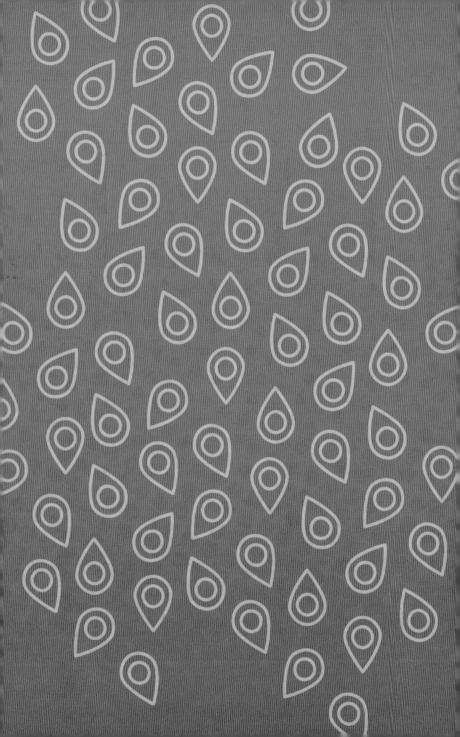

PITTSBURGH FOODIE FUNNIES

What's in the middle of a pierogi?

The letter "**R**"!

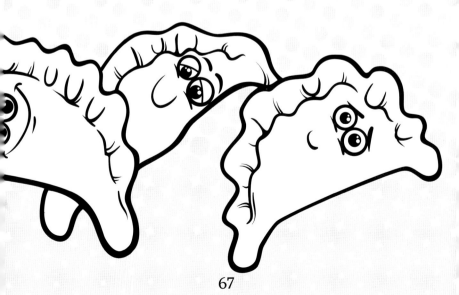

HOLD THE MAYO!

Fun Factoid:
In Pittsburgh,
they have
"chipped ham"
and call a sandwich
a "sammich!"

Delicious Factoid:

The famous Primanti Brothers sandwich chain
started in 1933 and was designed to feed truckers
who were making deliveries in the neighborhood.
The truckers had only one free hand when driving,
so the restaurant put the fries and coleslaw ON
the sandwich! An entire meal in one bite!

HOW DO YINZ LIKE DEM TOMATOES?

ORIGIN FACTOID:

H.J. Heinz went into business at eight years old, selling veggies from his mom's garden. Heinz ketchup was introduced in 1876.

SLOOOOOOW FACTOID:

Ketchup has been clocked coming slowly out of a Heinz bottle at 0.028 miles per hour.

Confusing Factoid:

Legend says that Henry John Heinz came up with ketchup by putting his own spin on an already popular tomato-based sauce that was derived from an old Chinese pickled fish sauce!

FUN FACTOID

The Senator John Heinz History Center is dedicated to Western Pennsylvania history and has cool vintage vehicles, including a trolley, fire engine . . . and a Heinz ketchup delivery truck!

KNOCK! KNOCK!

WHO'S THERE?
Ketchup!

KETCHUP WHO?
Ketchup with me, and you'll find out!

The banana split is said to have been first created at Tassell Pharmacy in nearby Latrobe, Pennsylvania, by David Strickler in 1904!

In honor of that, I present this a-peel-ing joke:

FACTOID DISPUTE:

The folks in Wilmington, Ohio, claim that native son Ernest Hazard invented the banana split in 1907. Thankfully, the National Ice Cream Retailers Association certified Latrobe as the birthplace, adding yet another sweet treat onto the Pittsburgh metro's repertoire!

In the 'Burgh, folks call soft drinks **"POP!"**

What do you call a chemist who invents sodas?

A fizzycist.

A REALLY BIG DILL!

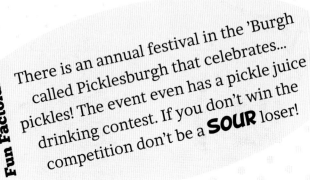

Fun Factoid: There is an annual festival in the 'Burgh called Picklesburgh that celebrates... pickles! The event even has a pickle juice drinking contest. If you don't win the competition don't be a **SOUR** loser!

Kosher Dill: Did you enjoy the Picklesburgh festival?

Gherkin: I RELISHED it!

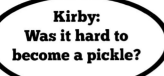

Kirby:
Was it hard to
become a pickle?

Cucumber:
Oh yes,
it was a jarring
experience!

Cornichon:
What do you say
when you start
playing a card game
with a pickle?

Bread and
Butter:
"Dill me in!"

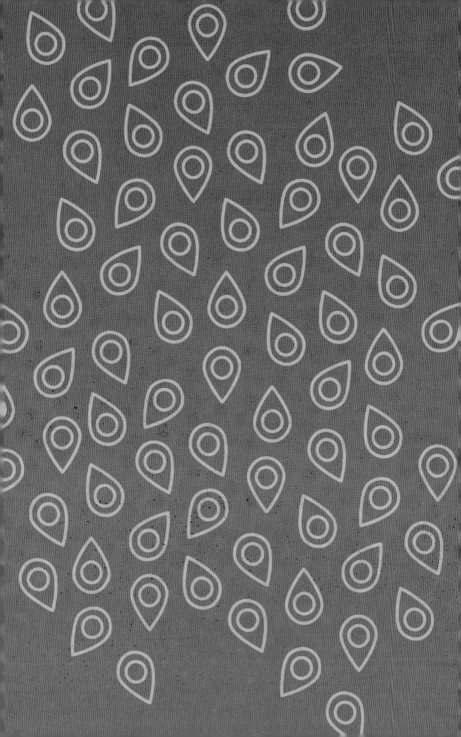

Pittsburgh is a city of champions. The Steel City's teams have won multiple Super Bowls, World Series, and Stanley Cup Championships. Go teams!

HUT, HUT, HIKE FACTOID:

The first professional football game was played in Pittsburgh in 1892. The game **PiTT**-ed local teams against each other: the Pittsburgh Athletic Club vs. the Allegheny Athletic Association. Allegheny won 4-0 to the thrill of the assembled Pittsburgh Athletic supporters!

ICY FACTOID:

Playing in 1901 and 1902, the Western Pennsylvania Hockey League (WPHL) was considered the first professional hockey league in the world.

The first true baseball stadium, Forbes Field, was built in 1909 in Pittsburgh.

 The first World Series was played in Pittsburgh in 1903, with the Pittsburgh Pirates losing to the Boston Americans. Those Boston Americans are full of beans!

HISTORICAL FACTOID

With not one but TWO of the greatest teams—the Pittsburgh Crawfords and the Homestead Grays—Pittsburgh was the grand slam of Negro League Baseball in the 1930s!

WHAT DID THE STEELER RECEIVER SAY TO THE FOOTBALL?

"CATCH YA LATER!"

What do a Pittsburgh Penguin and a magician have in common?

They both do hat tricks! (*)>

Why couldn't Cinderella make the Pittsburgh Riverhounds SC team?

Because she runs away from the ball!

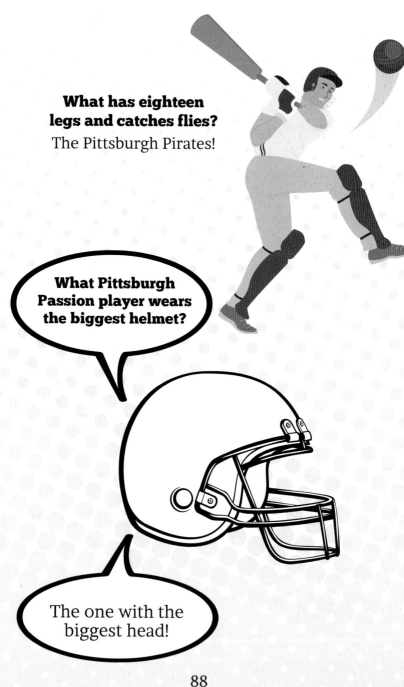

What has eighteen legs and catches flies?
The Pittsburgh Pirates!

What Pittsburgh Passion player wears the biggest helmet?

The one with the biggest head!

Why couldn't the Steel City Yellow Jackets player go on vacation?

He got called for traveling!

Why couldn't the marble player play in the championship?

He lost his marbles!

BLACK AND GOLD
NEVER GETS OLD!

Where do the Pittsburgh teams buy their new uniforms?

New **JERSEY**!

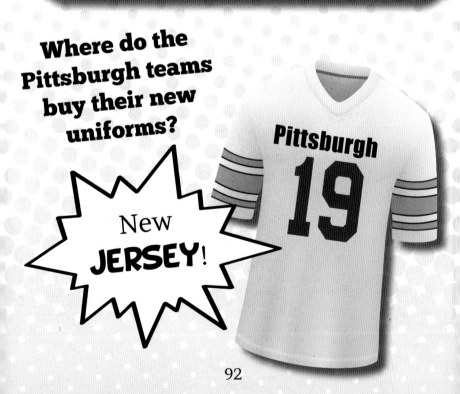

Pittsburgh
19

FORE! FACTOID:

The Grand View Golf Club actually sits on top of a mountain along the Monongahela River. Because of how challenging the course is, it is called "the Monster on the Mon!"

What do fish from the Monongahela use to get around the Grand View course?

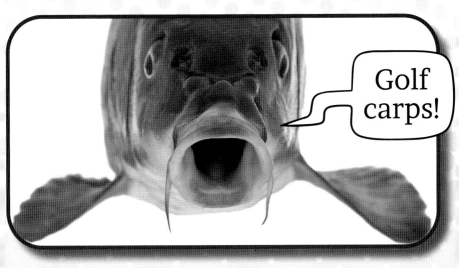

Golf carps!

One of a bunch of nicknames for Pittsburgh is "Sixburgh," coined after the Steelers' **SiX** Super Bowl wins. In the Steelers' honor, I share this classic number-six joke:

Why was 6 afraid of 7?

Because 7, 8, 9!

Another nickname for Pittsburgh is "the City of Champions," because of their awesome sports teams!

What do you get if you cross Pittsburgh with a barrel of monkeys?

The City of **CHIMP**-ions!